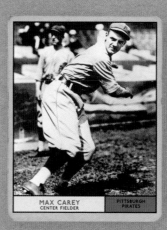
MAX CAREY
CENTER FIELDER
PITTSBURGH
PIRATES

WILLIE STARGELL
FIRST BASEMAN
PITTSBURGH
PIRATES

THE STORY OF THE PITTSBURGH PIRATES

Published by Creative Education
P.O. Box 227, Mankato, Minnesota 56002
Creative Education is an imprint of The Creative Company
www.thecreativecompany.us

Design and production by Blue Design
Art direction by Rita Marshall
Printed by Corporate Graphics in the United States of America

Photographs by Corbis (Bettmann, Underwood & Underwood), Getty Images (Bruce Bennett Studios, Mark Cunningham/MLB Photos, Diamond Images, Elsa, Focus on Sport, Leon Halip, Stan Honda/AFP, Kidwiler Collection/Diamond Images, Brad Mangin/MLB Photos, MLB Photos/MLB Photos, National Baseball Hall of Fame Library/MLB Photos, Christian Petersen, Rich Pilling/MLB Photos, Art Rickerby/Time & Life Pictures, Rogers Photo Archive, Mark Rucker/Transcendental Graphics, Klaus W. Saue, Jamie Squire, Rick Stewart, Jared Wickerham)

Library of Congress Cataloging-in-Publication Data

LeBoutillier, Nate.
The story of the Pittsburgh Pirates / by Nate LeBoutillier.
p. cm. — (Baseball: the great American game)
Includes index.
Summary: The history of the Pittsburgh Pirates professional baseball team from its inaugural 1882 season to today, spotlighting the team's greatest players and most memorable moments.
ISBN 978-1-60818-052-3
1. Pittsburgh Pirates (Baseball team)—History—Juvenile literature. I. Title. II. Title: Pittsburgh Pirates. III. Series.

GV875.P5L43 2011
796.357'640974886—dc22   2010025216

CPSIA: 110310 PO1381

First Edition
9 8 7 6 5 4 3 2 1

Page 3: Catcher Tony Peña
Page 4: Second baseman Akinori Iwamura

BASEBALL: THE GREAT AMERICAN GAME

THE STORY OF THE PITTSBURGH PIRATES

Nate LeBoutillier

CREATIVE EDUCATION

CONTENTS

STEELY RESOLVE

Pittsburgh, Pennsylvania, is known for its rivers. In the downtown area, the Allegheny and Monongahela rivers join to form the Ohio River at Point State Park. The Ohio River, in turn, feeds into the largest river system in the United States, the Mississippi. Starting in the late 19th century, Pittsburgh became known, too, as America's center for steel production. Hardworking people were needed to toil in Pittsburgh's busy steel mills, and the city earned wide and lasting renown for its work ethic.

But even hardworking people need a diversion, and baseball became Pittsburgh's pastime of choice in the late 1800s. Baseball "barnstorming," in which teams travel an area, finding opponents for games as they go, became a popular spectator sport in western Pennsylvania. The "Steel City" truly put down its baseball roots, though, in 1876, when a professional club called the Alleghenys was born. The franchise became known as the Pirates shortly after joining the National League (NL) in 1887, and a long and glorious baseball history began.

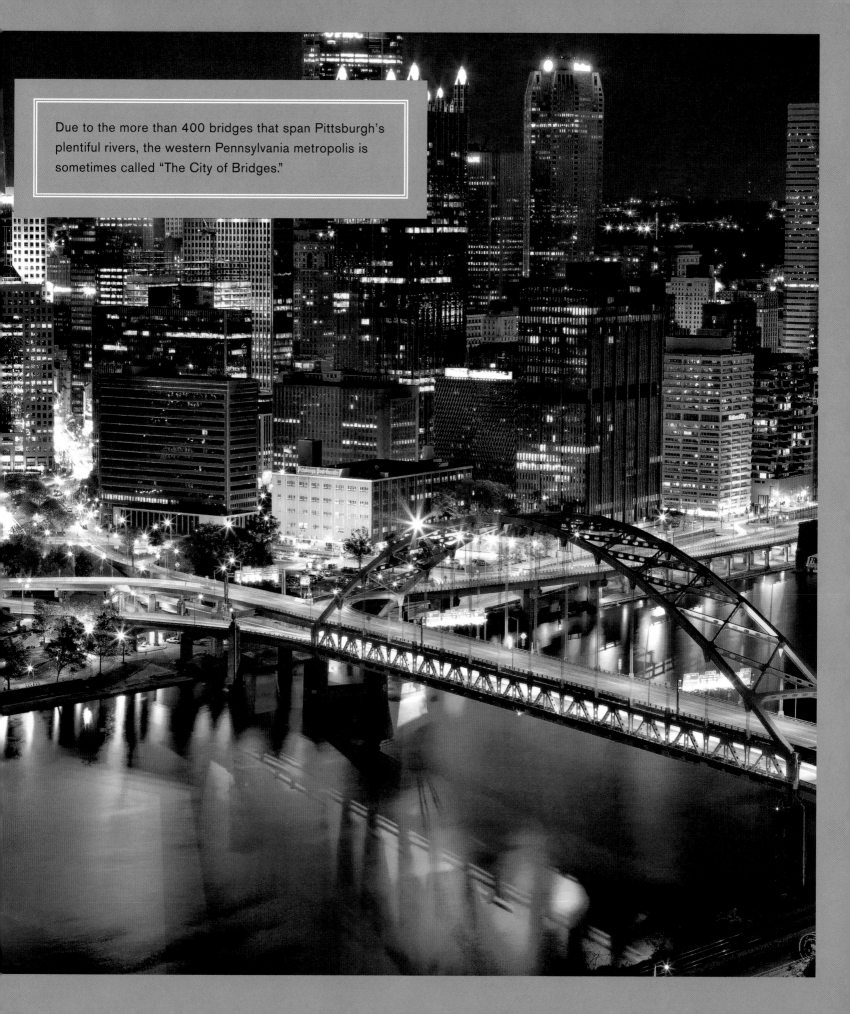

Due to the more than 400 bridges that span Pittsburgh's plentiful rivers, the western Pennsylvania metropolis is sometimes called "The City of Bridges."

PITCHER · WILBUR COOPER

Lefty Wilbur Cooper won 202 games in a Pirates uniform, more than any other pitcher in team history. Cooper had great control and was a fast worker on the mound, but his sidearm delivery seemed so effortless that some fans thought he wasn't giving a full effort. "Nothing could be further from the truth," wrote one sports reporter. "The Pirates southpaw works as hard as any other hurler, but his grace and ease of motion mislead some of the rooters." Cooper was also known for his fielding skill and a devastating pick-off move to third base that often nailed unsuspecting runners.

WILBUR COOPER
PITCHER

STATS

Pirates seasons: 1912–24

Height: 5-foot-11

Weight: 175

- 216–178 career record

- 4 seasons of 20-plus wins

- 279 career complete games

- 2.89 career ERA

The Alleghenys played in Pittsburgh's first professional game at Union Park on April 15, 1876. The club played in various leagues for a decade before the Alleghenys were invited to join the NL in 1887. A crowd 9,000 strong at Pittsburgh's Recreation Park watched the Alleghenys open their NL history by beating the league-champion Chicago White Stockings, 6–2. Leading the way in the team's early years was the talented battery of pitcher Pud Galvin and catcher Doggie Miller.

In 1890, many of the Alleghenys' best players jumped to the new Players League, only to see the organization disband after just one season. All of the players in the Players League were then expected to return to the teams they had played for in 1889. But in 1891, Pittsburgh signed second baseman Louis Bierbauer, who had previously suited up for the Philadelphia Athletics. Angry Athletics officials charged the Alleghenys with "pirating" away Bierbauer. Pittsburgh, instead of taking offense at the insult, not only kept the second baseman but embraced a new name, becoming the Pirates.

The Pirates struggled throughout the 1890s. But the arrival of shortstop Honus Wagner—known to fans as "The Flying Dutchman"—

FRED CLARKE

at the turn of the century changed the franchise's fortunes. In 1900, Wagner led the NL with a .381 batting average and hit 45 doubles and 22 triples. One reporter wrote, "He walks like a crab, fields like an octopus, and hits like the devil."

The Pirates won three straight NL pennants from 1901 to 1903 behind the play of Wagner, pitcher Charles "Deacon" Phillippe, and outfielder and manager Fred Clarke. After the Pirates' third pennant, club president Barney Dreyfuss challenged the Boston Pilgrims—winners of the American League (AL) pennant—to a best-of-nine world championship series, and thus the first World Series was born. Although the Pirates managed to defeat Boston's ace pitcher, the immortal Cy Young, in the first game of the series, the Pilgrims won the trophy, five games to three.

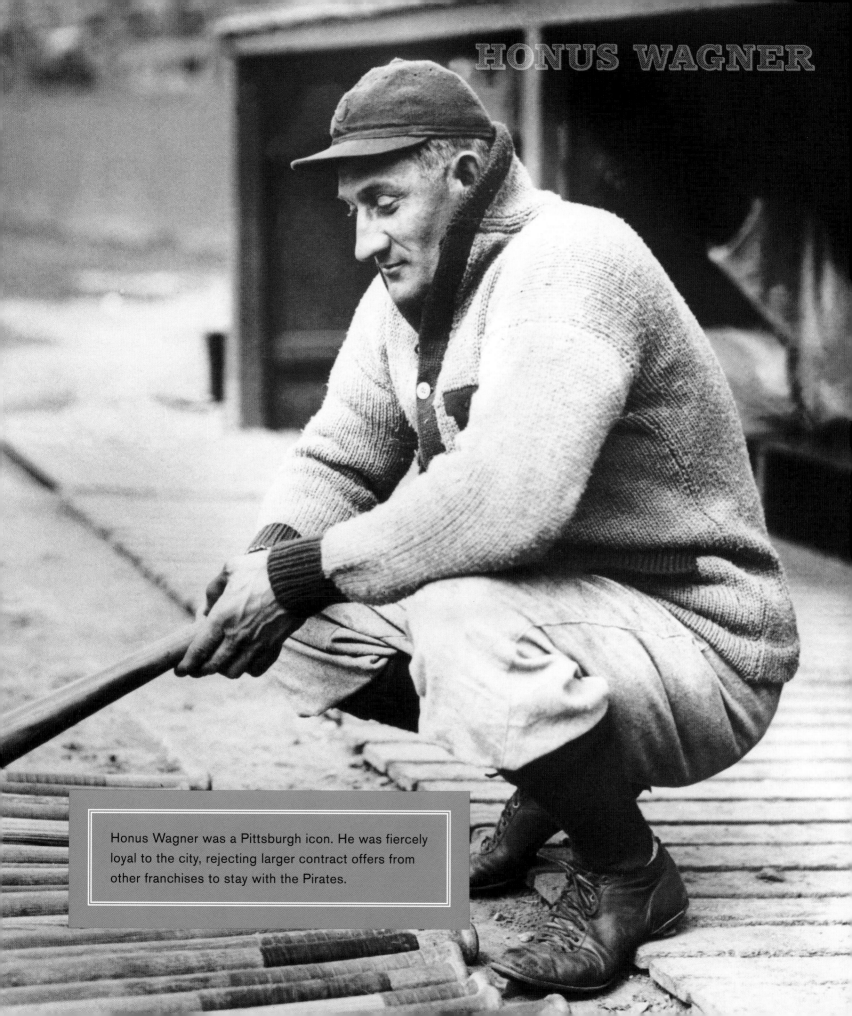

Honus Wagner was a Pittsburgh icon. He was fiercely loyal to the city, rejecting larger contract offers from other franchises to stay with the Pirates.

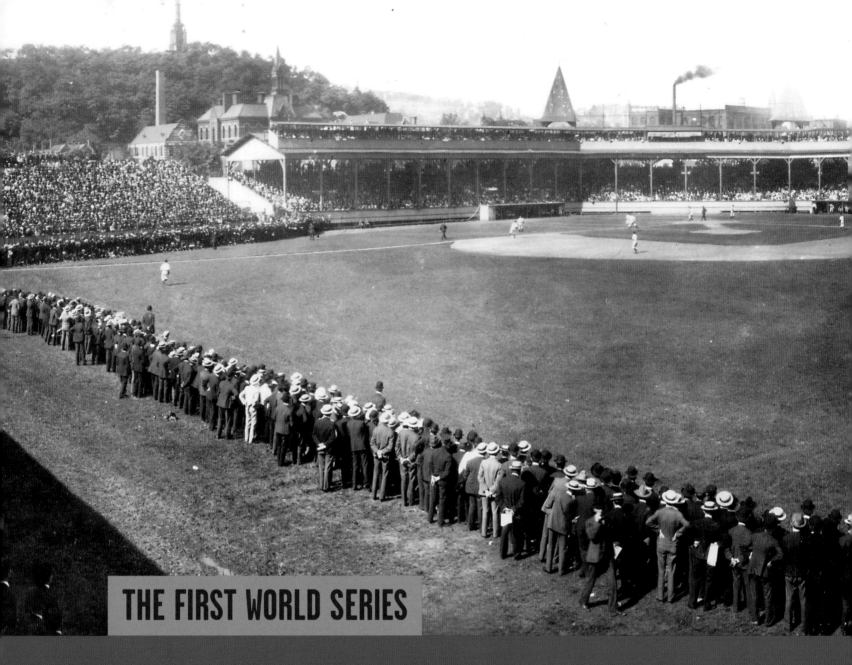

THE FIRST WORLD SERIES

When Pittsburgh Pirates owner Barney Dreyfuss proposed holding the first World Series after the 1903 season, he primarily had business interests in mind. In his letter to the owner of the Boston Pilgrims, Dreyfuss wrote that a championship competition "would create great interest in baseball, in our leagues, and in our players. I also believe it would be a financial success." Dreyfuss was right. Overflow crowds came to each game in the series, benefiting the owners as well as scalpers, who bought tickets for as little as $1 each and resold them for $5 to $10 on the street. Every seat was filled for each game, and hundreds of fans stood in the back of the outfield. A rule was made that any ball hit into the crowd on the field would be an automatic triple. The teams combined for 25 triples in the series, which will forever stand as a World Series record. The owners also agreed to share their profits from the gate receipts with the players—a practice that is still followed today. The winning Pilgrims received checks in the amount of $1,182 per player for their efforts.

CATCHER · TONY PEÑA

When they were growing up in the Dominican Republic, Tony Peña and his brother Ramón (who became a minor-league pitcher in the Pirates organization) learned to play baseball from their mother, a former softball star. She taught Tony to set up behind the plate in an unusual crouch with one leg extended to the side. From that position, Peña was able to both block wild pitches effectively and to rise up quickly to throw out would-be base stealers. Tony's fielding skills and timely hitting helped him become a five-time All-Star. After his playing career, he managed the Kansas City Royals for four seasons.

TONY PEÑA
CATCHER

PITTSBURGH
PIRATES

STATS

Pirates seasons: 1980–86

Height: 6 feet

Weight: 180

- 708 career RBI

- 5-time All-Star

- 4-time Gold Glove winner

- 11,212 career putouts

PIRATES

FIRST BASEMAN · WILLIE STARGELL

Pirates manager Chuck Tanner once said, "When you had Willie Stargell on your team, it was like having a 10-karat diamond on your finger." With his talent and leadership, "Pops" was the Pirates' most valuable player on and off the field. Stargell was a scary presence at the plate. He would twirl his heavy bat in a sweeping windmill motion as he settled in to face the pitcher. Then he would stride powerfully into the pitch and frequently send the ball soaring high and far. A 12-foot-tall statue of Stargell today stands outside Pittsburgh's PNC Park, as befits a man who often seemed much larger than life.

WILLIE STARGELL
FIRST BASEMAN

STATS

Pirates seasons: 1962–82

Height: 6-foot-2

Weight: 225

- 475 career HR

- 1979 NL co-MVP

- 7-time All-Star

- Baseball Hall of Fame inductee (1988)

PIE AND POISON

n 1909, Pittsburgh returned to the World Series after winning a club-record 110 games. The series that year was billed as a marquee matchup between Wagner and Detroit Tigers outfielder Ty Cobb, the AL's best hitter. But the real star turned out to be rookie Pirates pitcher Charles "Babe" Adams, who tossed three complete-game victories to lead the Pirates to a four-games-to-three series triumph and their first world championship.

After that 1909 title run, the Pirates slowly faded in the NL standings as the great players of their pennant-winning teams grew old. It would take club management a decade to build a big winner again, despite the efforts of star pitcher Wilbur Cooper and speedy outfielder Max "Scoops" Carey, who routinely led the NL in steals. Pittsburgh's fortunes finally began to change for the better in the early 1920s with the arrival of third baseman Harold "Pie" Traynor. An outstanding all-around player, Traynor was equally skilled at the plate and in the field. "He had the quickest hands and the quickest arms of any third baseman I ever saw," said Pirates first baseman Charlie Grimm.

Traynor solidified the Pirates' defense and joined with Carey and speedy outfielder Kiki Cuyler to give Pittsburgh the top offense in the league. In 1925, the Pirates raced to another NL pennant, leading the league in runs scored, hits, doubles, triples, and steals. The Pirates got off to a slow start in the World Series against the Washington Senators, losing three of the first four games. Then they stormed back with two wins to even the series. In Game 7, Pittsburgh fell behind again before rallying in the eighth inning against Hall of Fame Senators pitcher Walter Johnson to capture the championship.

Over the next two seasons, Traynor was joined in Pittsburgh by a pair of hard-hitting outfielders—the Waner brothers. As a rookie in 1926, right fielder Paul Waner did two important things for the Pirates. He posted a terrific .336 average, and he told the team's owner, "My younger brother Lloyd is an even better player than I am. You'd better grab him." Luckily, the Pirates took his advice. For the next decade, the Waner brothers were the heart of Pittsburgh's offense. They earned the nicknames "Big Poison" and "Little Poison" because they were murder on opposing pitchers, and each would later be inducted into the Hall of Fame.

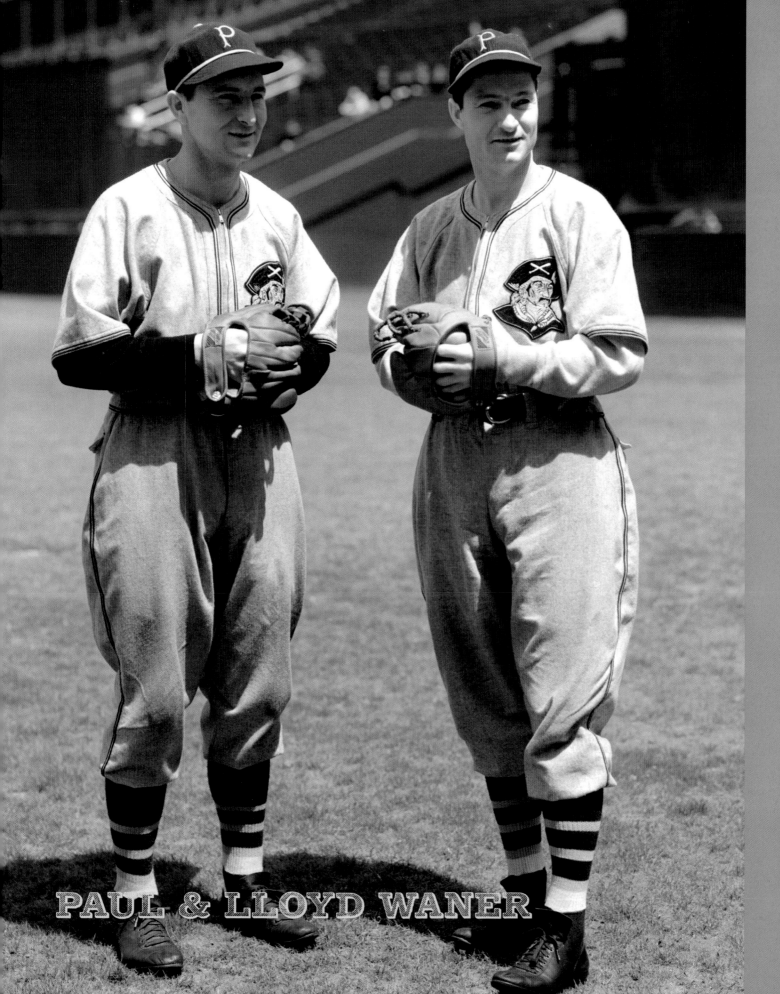

PAUL & LLOYD WANER

SECOND BASEMAN · BILL MAZEROSKI

Some baseball experts consider Bill Mazeroski the best-fielding second baseman of all time. His quick hands enabled him to establish a major-league career record for turning double plays (1,706). He is even more famous for the clutch home run he hit to win the 1960 World Series. But "Maz" brought something special to the Pirates that went beyond batting or fielding. Said Pirates pitcher Steve Blass: "They can talk about all the great Pirates—and there have been a lot of them. But Maz represented the spirit of Pittsburgh and the Pirates better than any of them."

STATS

Pirates seasons: 1956–72

Height: 5-foot-11

Weight: 183

- 2,016 career hits

- 8-time Gold Glove winner

- 7-time All-Star

- Baseball Hall of Fame inductee (2001)

BILL MAZEROSKI
SECOND BASEMAN

Pie and the Poisons led the Pirates to another pennant in 1927, but Pittsburgh was no match for the New York Yankees' legendary "Murderers' Row" lineup in the World Series. Some writers claimed the Pirates became intimidated before the first pitch was even thrown, watching Babe Ruth and other Yankees sluggers slam ball after ball out of the park during batting practice. The Yankees swept the series in four games.

The Pirates remained in the hunt for another pennant throughout the rest of the 1920s and '30s, but they never finished higher than second place. Pittsburgh fans continued to hope for another championship as they watched some outstanding talent perform in the Steel City. Among the best players during those seasons was shortstop Arky Vaughan, who arrived in 1932 and batted over .300 in each of his 10 seasons in Pittsburgh black and gold.

Yet despite all their offensive talent, the Pirates fell short year after year. "Gee that was tough to take," Paul Waner later said. "We had good teams, too. You know, Pie, Arky, and me and Lloyd—all good players. But we never quite made it. It'd just tear you apart."

PIRATES

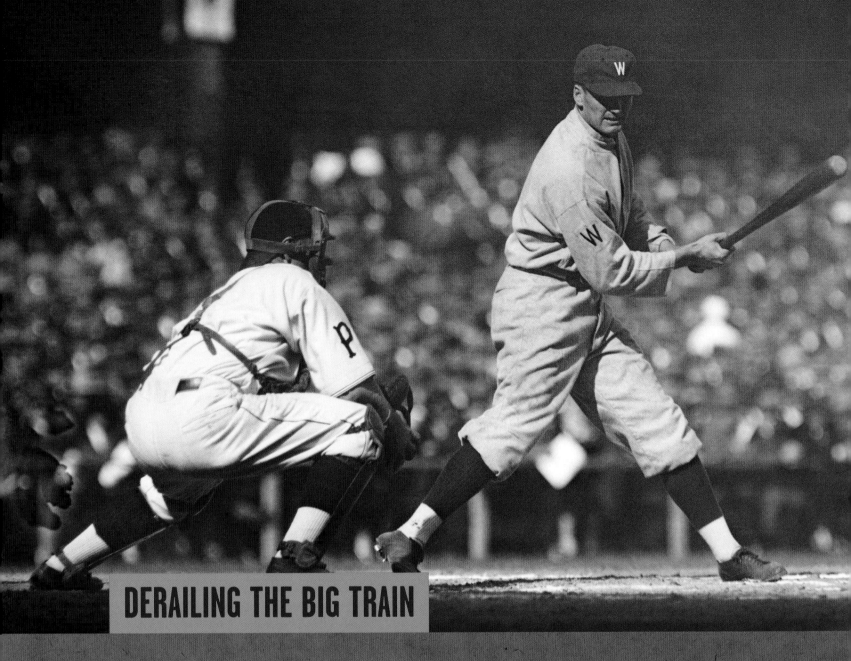

DERAILING THE BIG TRAIN

The 1925 World Series was billed as a battle between the best-hitting team in the NL—the Pirates—and arguably the best pitcher in AL history, Walter Johnson of the Washington Senators. The Pirates' starting lineup had batted an amazing .324 in 1925, while Johnson, known as "The Big Train" because of his locomotivelike fastball, had been a 20-game winner for the 12th time in his career. Johnson shut down the Pirates' bats in Games 1 and 4, holding Pittsburgh to 1 run and 11 hits altogether. The Pirates battled back to win Games 5 and 6 but faced two major hurdles going into Game 7. For one thing, no team had ever come back from a three-games-to-one deficit to win a World Series before. And for another, they would be facing Johnson again. When the Senators got off to a 4–0 lead in the top of the first inning, Pirates fans feared the worst. But Johnson didn't have his best stuff that day, and the Pirates trailed only 7–6 when they batted in the bottom of the eighth. Pittsburgh then capitalized on sloppy Senators fielding to score two unearned runs against Johnson and clinch its second world championship.

PIRATE POWER

uring the 1940s, the Pirates were an average team with one real star—slugging outfielder Ralph Kiner, who won the NL home run crown a record seven seasons in a row with his swashbuckling swing. But even Kiner's long balls couldn't keep the team from spiraling downhill during the early 1950s. The Pirates lost more than 100 games each year in 1952, 1953, and 1954, finishing dead last in the NL all 3 seasons.

Pittsburgh fans were upset, but general manager Branch Rickey had a rebuilding plan. He began trading away veterans and bringing in talented young players such as shortstop Dick Groat, relief pitcher Elroy Face, and slugging first baseman Dick Stuart, whose fielding difficulties earned him the nickname "Dr. Strangeglove." In a final brilliant move before the 1955 season, Rickey signed a young Puerto Rican outfielder named Roberto Clemente away from the Brooklyn Dodgers. Clemente would become the Pirates' steadiest star for the next 18 years.

Rickey's rebuilding plan took longer than he expected, but by 1960, all the pieces were in place for Pittsburgh to make another

DICK GROAT

run at an NL pennant. During that magical season, everything seemed to go right for the Pirates. The team compiled a 95–59 record to capture its first pennant in 33 years; Groat was named the league's Most Valuable Player (MVP); Clemente batted a solid .314; and pitcher Vernon Law earned the NL Cy Young Award as the league's best pitcher with a 20–9 record.

The glue holding the Pirates together, however, was second baseman Bill Mazeroski. "Maz" was a natural leader and a steadying influence on the rest of the players. He was also one of the finest-fielding second-sackers of all time. Describing how Mazeroski handled the pivot on a double play, Groat said, "It was as if his hands never touched the ball. As soon as the ball touched his glove, it was on its way to first base. Frankly, I never saw anything like it."

Maz earned a prominent place in Pirates history with his

PIRATES

THIRD BASEMAN · PIE TRAYNOR

Harold "Pie" Traynor was one of baseball's finest fielders at the hot corner. He had great reflexes and made an art of diving for balls to his right to stop sure base hits and then firing bullets across the diamond to first. A Pittsburgh sportswriter once reported, "The batter doubled down the left-field foul line, but Traynor threw him out." Traynor was an outstanding hitter as well, and his .320 lifetime batting average is the second-best ever by a third-sacker (after Boston Red Sox star Wade Boggs). Traynor almost always put the ball in play, striking out an average of only 16 times per year during his career.

PIE TRAYNOR
THIRD BASEMAN

PITTSBURGH
PIRATES

STATS

Pirates seasons: 1920–35, 1937

Height: 6 feet

Weight: 170

- 1,273 career RBI

- .320 career BA

- 2-time All-Star

- Baseball Hall of Fame inductee (1948)

HARVEY HADDIX

ALMOST PERFECT

On May 26, 1959, Pirates left-hander Harvey Haddix pitched the best game ever thrown in major-league history—and lost. Haddix had everything going right against the Milwaukee Braves that night. In the clubhouse before the game, Haddix had discussed how he planned to pitch to each Braves batter. Third baseman Don Hoak said, "Harv, if you pitch the way you say you will, you'll have a no-hitter." After nine innings, Haddix was doing even better than that; he was hurling a perfect game. Twenty-seven Braves batters had come to the plate, and all had made outs.

But the game still wasn't over, because the Pirates hadn't scored yet, either. With two outs in the top of the 10th, Pittsburgh first baseman Dick Stuart hit a shot that looked like it would clear the fence, but the wind held it up for a long out. If Haddix was upset, he didn't show it. He just kept mowing down the Braves in order in the 10th, 11th, and 12th innings. Then, in the bottom of the 13th, a Hoak throwing error ended the perfect game. That runner later scored, giving Milwaukee a 1–0 win. For Harvey Haddix, being almost perfect wasn't good enough.

performance in the 1960 World Series against the Yankees. The battle between the league champs came down to the bottom of the ninth inning of Game 7 with the score tied 9–9. Maz led off for the Pirates and tried to relax at the plate. "On my previous at bat, I had overswung and grounded out," he later recalled. "I wanted to make certain I didn't do the same thing again." Maz took one pitch for a ball. Then he slammed the next offering over the left-field wall to secure the championship for the Pirates. Outside Pittsburgh's Forbes Field, cars honked, trolley cars clanged, and jubilant Pirates fans danced in the streets. The Pirates were on top again.

Pittsburgh's celebration was short-lived, however. The next year, the Pirates fell to a disappointing sixth place, and the club would remain in the middle of the league standings throughout most of the 1960s. First baseman and future team captain Willie Stargell, who joined the Pirates in 1962, explained Pittsburgh's problem. "The spark had disappeared from the club . . . the magic had passed," he said. "All that remained were 25 talented ballplayers not good enough to win a pennant."

The most talented player of the group—and the most misunderstood—

was Clemente. A man of great pride and honesty, Clemente felt he never received the respect he deserved because he was Latin American and had difficulty speaking English. There was no denying his skill on the field, though. During his career in Pittsburgh, Clemente compiled a lifetime batting average of .317 and earned 12 consecutive Gold Glove awards for his outstanding fielding.

Clemente saved his best performance for the 1971 World Series, when a reinvigorated Pirates squad made an unlikely run back to the "Fall Classic," where it took on and defeated the Baltimore Orioles. With fans throughout America and beyond watching him on television, Clemente batted .414 in the series, made several spectacular catches in the field, ran the bases with abandon, and was the unanimous choice as series MVP.

Sadly, that was one of Clemente's last shining moments. In December 1972, he died in a plane crash on his way to deliver medicine and supplies to victims of a terrible earthquake in Nicaragua. At Clemente's funeral, Puerto Rican governor Rafael Hernandez Colon said, "Our youth lose an idol. Our people lose one of their glories."

The Pirates have won five world championships, but none was as dramatic as the 1960 title, won on Bill Mazeroski's unforgettable walk-off home run.

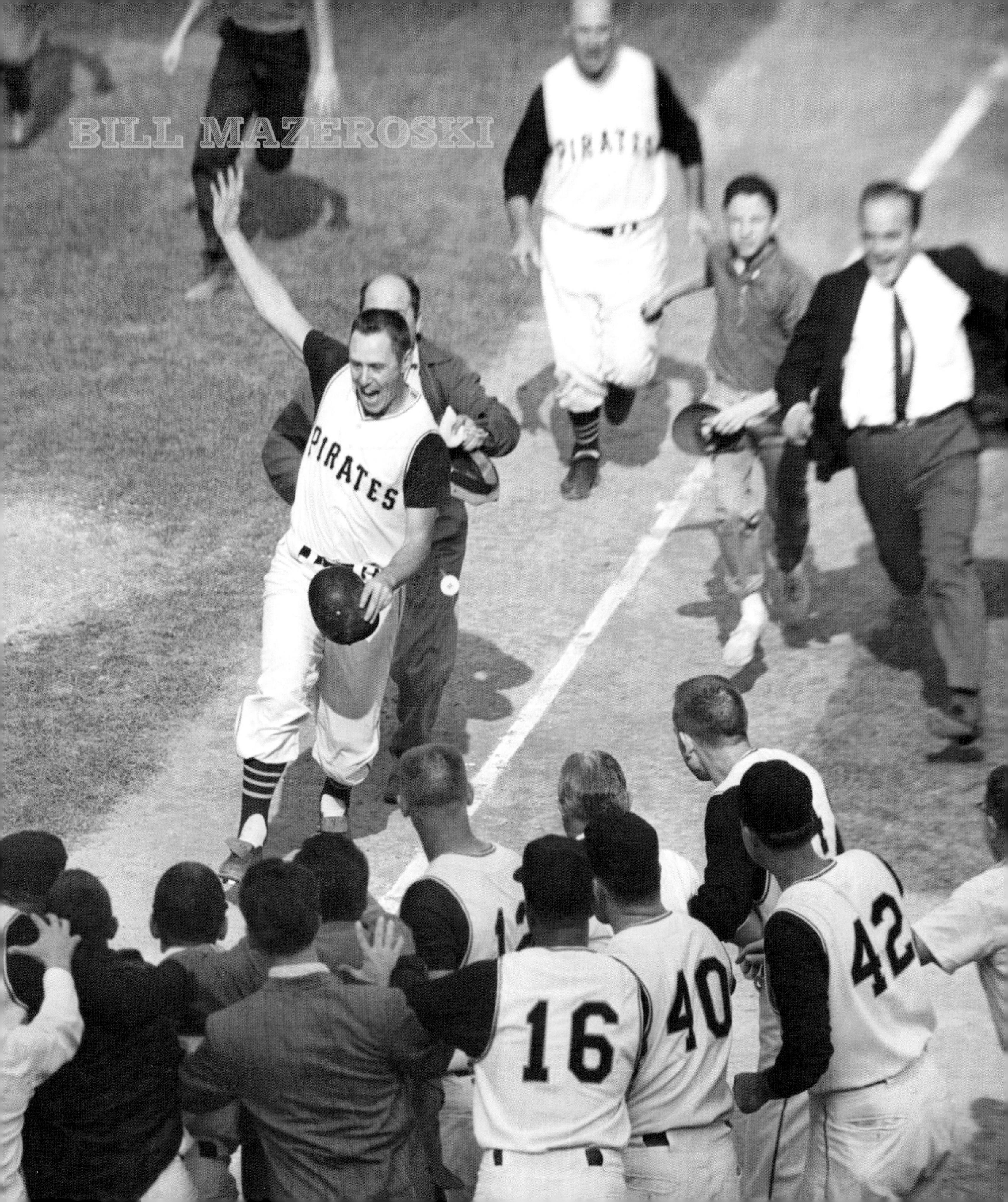

BILL MAZEROSKI

SHORTSTOP · HONUS WAGNER

John Peter "Honus" Wagner spent 57 years in a Pirates uniform—18 as a player and 39 as a coach. He was the team's first great star and still holds club records for triples and runs scored. Wagner earned the nickname "The Flying Dutchman" because of his speed on the bases and his German heritage. He had huge hands and sometimes scooped up dirt and pebbles along with grounders and threw them all toward first base for the out. Wagner was among five players elected to the Hall of Fame in its first year of existence.

STATS

Pirates seasons: 1900–17

Height: 5-foot-11

Weight: 200

- 3,420 career hits
- 252 career triples
- 8-time NL leader in BA
- Baseball Hall of Fame inductee (1936)

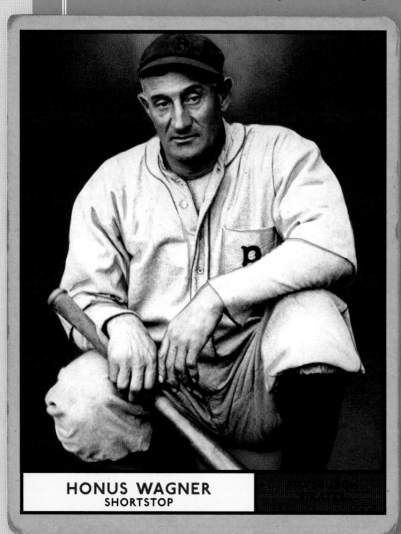

HONUS WAGNER
SHORTSTOP

FAMILY TIME

ith Clemente gone, the mantle of team leadership passed to Stargell, who inspired his teammates with his hard work and sense of humor. He made a special point of "adopting" younger players such as outfielders Dave Parker and Al Oliver and third baseman Bill Madlock, earning him the nickname "Pops." Pops Stargell created a close-knit Pirates family that started to win big again in the late 1970s. In 1979, the Pirates rose all the way to the top once more.

That year, Stargell chose a theme song for the team, a disco tune called "We Are Family," and requested that it be played at all home games in the club's park, Three Rivers Stadium. "That song not only brought us and the fans closer together," Stargell recalled, "but it became a rallying cry for the city as well. We were all one. . . . Pittsburghers all moved to the same beat."

That beat was a winning one. The Pirates edged by the Montreal Expos for the NL Eastern Division crown during the regular season. (The league had been split into two divisions in 1969.) Then they swept

WILLIE STARGELL

the Cincinnati Reds in the NL Championship Series (NLCS) to earn a spot in the World Series opposite the Orioles, the team they had defeated in 1971. Just as in 1971, the series went a full seven games. In the finale, Pops Stargell pounded four hits, including a go-ahead home run, to lead his family to victory.

In the early 1980s, the Pirates family broke up. Stargell retired, and most of Pittsburgh's other stars moved on to new teams, leaving the club with little talent besides catcher Tony Peña. The Pirates sat at the bottom of the NL East by 1984, but luckily, help was on the way. General manager Syd Thrift promoted two young outfielders, Barry Bonds and Bobby Bonilla, from the club's minor-league system in 1986. Then he made some wily trades for pitchers Doug Drabek and Neal Heaton. Thrift asked Pittsburgh fans to be patient while these young players developed, and that patience was soon rewarded.

In 1988, the Pirates surprised most fans by making a strong run at the division title before losing out to the New York Mets late in the season. The club suffered through

Famed for his towering home runs, Willie Stargell was known to warm up in the on-deck circle by swinging a sledgehammer instead of the typical weighted bat.

LEFT FIELDER · RALPH KINER

No player except Babe Ruth ever dominated home run hitting the way Ralph Kiner did from 1946 to 1952: he led the league in homers his first seven seasons in Pittsburgh. Kiner hit home runs in streaks, once clubbing eight in a four-game span. Unfortunately, he was the Pirates' only real offensive weapon during the late 1940s. Once, when Kiner threatened to hold out for more money, the Pirates' owner told him, "We finished last with you in the lineup. How much worse could we do without you?" After his playing days ended, Kiner spent many years as an announcer with the New York Mets.

RALPH KINER
LEFT FIELDER

PITTSBURGH PIRATES

STATS

Pirates seasons: 1946–53

Height: 6-foot-2

Weight: 195

- **369 career HR**

- **1,015 career RBI**

- **6-time All-Star**

- **Baseball Hall of Fame inductee (1975)**

THE OUTFIELD OF DREAMS

In 1989, a baseball movie called *Field of Dreams* did big business at the box office. That same year, Pirates manager Jim Leyland put together what became known in Pittsburgh as the "Outfield of Dreams"—Barry Bonds in left field, Andy van Slyke (pictured, right) in center, and Bobby Bonilla in right. No NL team could match the Pirates' trio in the field or at bat. All three made All-Star teams while playing in Pittsburgh. They powered the Pirates to NL East titles in both 1990 and 1991, smacking a combined 142 home runs and driving in 610 runs during the 2 seasons. Bonds and van Slyke also garnered Gold Glove awards both years for their stellar fielding, and Bonds and Bonilla ranked first and second in the voting for NL MVP in 1990. "I wish I could split the award and give half to Bobby," Bonds said at the award ceremony. "He's just as much an MVP as I am." But as good as they were during the regular season, the dream outfielders seemed to fizzle in the playoffs, and their inability to get big hits during NLCS games proved to be a nightmare for Pirates fans.

injuries in 1989 but was back and better than ever in 1990. This time the Pirates caught and then passed the Mets in September to win the NL East. The Pirates were hot, but they couldn't match the even hotter Reds in the NLCS and lost the series in six games.

Despite the postseason defeat, that 1990 season gave new hope to the Pittsburgh faithful. Bonds earned the NL MVP award by batting .301 and compiling 33 homers, 114 runs batted in (RBI), and 52 stolen bases. Bonilla was close behind in the MVP voting, and Drabek won the Cy Young Award, going 22–6 while walking only 56 batters in 33 starts.

The Pirates won a second consecutive NL East title in 1991, but they came up short once again in the NLCS, losing to the Atlanta Braves in a tight, seven-game series. The same two clubs repeated as division champs in 1992 and faced off in another nail-biting NLCS. This time, the turning point was a three-run Atlanta rally in the bottom of the ninth inning of Game 7 that left the Pirates and their fans stunned. "We were so close," lamented Pirates shortstop Jay Bell. "I really can't believe it happened still."

CENTER FIELDER · MAX CAREY

It was said that the only thing that covered more grass in center field of Pittsburgh's Forbes Field than Max Carey was the smoke from the local steel mills. Carey set league records for putouts and assists by an outfielder, and while he may have been only a slightly-better-than-average hitter, he was absolute lightning on the base paths. Carey was one of the heroes for the Pirates in the 1925 World Series, when, despite suffering from a broken rib, he batted .458, stole three bases, and got four hits off Washington Senators ace Walter Johnson in the deciding Game 7.

MAX CAREY
CENTER FIELDER

PITTSBURGH
PIRATES

STATS

Pirates seasons: 1910–26

Height: 5-foot-11

Weight: 170

- **2,665 career hits**

- **738 stolen bases**

- **10-time NL leader in steals**

- **Baseball Hall of Fame inductee (1961)**

Although he would bulk up to 230 pounds later in his career, Barry Bonds was a 185-pound speedster during his seasons with the Pirates.

That loss to the Braves signaled the start of a depressing slide in Pittsburgh. The team had already lost Bonilla to free agency in 1991. Shortly after the 1992 postseason, the cash-strapped Pirates were unable to match contracts offered to Bonds and Drabek by other teams. With its lineup suddenly depleted, the Pirates plummeted in the NL East. A promising era in Pittsburgh had come to an end.

WAITING FOR A WINNER

 ins were hard to come by in Pittsburgh during the rest of the 1990s. As the team declined in the standings, attendance also decreased at Three Rivers Stadium, and an unfortunate cycle took hold. Lower attendance meant that less money was available to sign or develop players who could improve the team's performance on the field. Things got so bad that there was even talk of moving the Pirates from Pittsburgh to northern Virginia. Luckily, in February 1996, newspaper mogul Kevin McClatchy bought the team, vowing to keep the franchise in Pittsburgh and to help it become competitive again.

BARRY BONDS

Inspired by the new owner's confidence, the Pirates made a strong run in 1997. Led by speedy second baseman Tony Womack, veteran outfielder Al Martin, and tough catcher Jason Kendall, the Pirates battled for the NL Central Division lead all season and finished in second place at a surprising 79–83. "A lot of people said we would be a joke," said Womack. "But if we can keep this group of guys together and

JASON BAY

ELUSIVE HONOR

Over the years, Pirates stars have won a multitude of honors—MVP awards, Gold Gloves, and Cy Young Awards. But no Pirates newcomer had ever been named NL Rookie of the Year. That finally changed in 2004 when outfielder Jason Bay captured the award by hitting .282 with 26 homers and 82 RBI. Bay had the double distinction of also being the first Canadian-born player to receive the honor. "The award means the world to me," Bay said. "You walk into the locker room here and see all those jerseys [of past Pirates greats] hanging up. It's kind of amazing it never happened before." Why had the award eluded so many Pirates stars of earlier eras? It was first presented in 1947, so players such as Honus Wagner, Pie Traynor, and Paul Waner could not have won. Even Ralph Kiner, who led the NL in homers during his rookie season in 1946, started his career a year too early. In 1955, Roberto Clemente lost out to St. Louis Cardinals rookie Bill Virdon, who later played center field next to Clemente in the Pittsburgh outfield. In 1963, Willie Stargell finished behind Pete Rose of the Cincinnati Reds, and in 1986, Barry Bonds came in sixth in the award voting.

RIGHT FIELDER · ROBERTO CLEMENTE

Roberto Clemente could turn any pitch—even ones at ankle height or nearly over his head—into a base hit. He was a free swinger who nearly always made contact with the ball. Clemente was also the best right fielder of his era, with a rocket arm that struck fear into base runners. But he is just as well known for his humanitarian efforts, including the charity mission to Nicaragua that cost him his life. Clemente once said, "Any time you have an opportunity to make a difference in this world and you don't, then you are wasting your time on Earth."

ROBERTO CLEMENTE
RIGHT FIELDER

PITTSBURGH
PIRATES

STATS

Pirates seasons: 1955–72

Height: 5-foot-11

Weight: 175

- **1,305 career RBI**

- **3,000 career hits**

- **12-time All-Star**

- **Baseball Hall of Fame inductee (1973)**

MANAGER · FRED CLARKE

In 1897, 24-year-old outfielder Fred Clarke was named player/manager of his club, the Louisville Colonels. Despite the added responsibility, Clarke hit a career-best .390 that year. Then, in 1900, he was traded to Pittsburgh, where he took over the reins of the Pirates. In the Steel City, Clarke continued to star on the field and to drive the Pirates to victory after victory as manager. Clarke's Pittsburgh teams topped the NL four times between 1901 and 1909 and competed in two World Series. Clarke completed his playing career with a .312 lifetime batting average and his managing career with a .576 winning percentage.

STATS

Pirates seasons as player/ manager: 1900–15

Managerial record: 1,602–1,181

World Series championship: 1909

Baseball Hall of Fame inductee (1945)

FRED CLARKE
MANAGER

add another bat or two, we'll be doing the laughing."

Unfortunately, injuries and continuing financial problems kept laughs to a minimum in Pittsburgh. But McClatchy had another idea that could revitalize the club and its fans as the new millennium approached. In April 1999, construction began on a stadium that would be called PNC Park. Two years later, the Pirates moved into their new home—one of the most beautiful in all of major league baseball. More than 2.4 million fans filled up PNC Park in 2001, thrilled by its dramatic views of the expanding Pittsburgh skyline and reminders of past Pirates glory in the form of statues of Honus Wagner, Roberto Clemente, and Willie Stargell.

Although the stadium was a hit with Pirates fans, the play on the field was not. It seemed like every time a Pittsburgh player's star began to rise, the team would trade him or lose him through free agency. By 2006, the Pirates had accumulated a promising lineup that included pitchers Zach Duke and Ian Snell, All-Star outfielder Jason Bay, young catcher Ronny Paulino, and sweet-swinging infielder Freddy Sanchez. They even hosted the midseason All-Star Game at PNC Park. But the team ended 2006 with

IAN SNELL

the same dismal mark it had recorded the previous season: 67–95, good for last place in the NL Central.

The Pirates improved their record in 2007—but only by a single game. Then, in 2008, after another lackluster start, the destructive cycle began to play out again. The team started trading away its best players to reduce payroll and launch a new rebuilding effort, and the Pirates maddeningly slid to a 67–95 finish again. The 2009 season saw Pittsburgh deal away nearly its entire starting infield in Sanchez, shortstop Jack Wilson, and first baseman Adam LaRoche, along with All-Star outfielder Nate McLouth. The roster purge resulted in a 62–99 mark and a 17th consecutive losing season, which put the Pirates in the record books with the longest losing drought by any professional sports team in the history of North America.

Pirates general manager Neal Huntington responded to Pittsburgh fans' justifiable complaints with both humor and honesty, saying, "It's not like we're breaking up the '27 Yankees. These aren't easy moves to make. However, the goal here is to build a winning organization." Although the misery continued in 2010 with a major-league-worst 57–

1911
HONUS WAGNER
PSA
PR-1
09061520

A COSTLY CARD

Kids (and grown-up kids) have been collecting baseball cards practically since the beginning of the professional game. When an anonymous collector bought an Honus Wagner baseball card for $2.8 million in 2007, it easily reset the record for the most valuable baseball card of all time. Unbeknownst to Wagner, a hard-hitting but clean-living Pirates shortstop, the American Tobacco Company had begun producing the card in 1910. But the card was discontinued after Wagner objected, stating that he didn't want children collecting the card to associate him—or themselves—with tobacco products. As a result, only about 50 of the cards were produced, and although a number have turned up over the years to be bought and sold at various auctions, finding a card in "mint condition" was a rare event indeed. One such card was purchased by legendary hockey player Wayne Gretzky in 1991. Gretzky, in turn, sold the card for half a million dollars, and the card changed hands multiple times before it eventually generated the record $2.8-million payday. "Some people have referred to it as the *Mona Lisa* of baseball cards," said Dan Imler, a baseball card auctioneer. "Somebody who desires to own the very best of something, this is it."

ANDREW McCUTCHEN

Andrew McCutchen showed signs of stardom in 2010, hitting 16 home runs, stealing 33 bases, and displaying great range in center field.

GARRETT JONES

Pittsburgh fans cheered the run production of first baseman Garrett Jones (opposite) and the dependable defense of shortstop Ronny Cedeño (below).

RONNY CEDEÑO

105 finish, swift center fielder Andrew McCutchen, steady-hitting left fielder Jose Tabata, and slugging first baseman Garrett Jones offered some hope of a long-awaited turnaround in Pittsburgh.

The Pirates' descent from steady contender into perennial doormat has not been a pretty sight for Pittsburgh's baseball fans, especially as other local pro teams—including football's Steelers and hockey's Penguins—have achieved championship glory in their respective sports. Still, as today's Pirates battle on in PNC Park, their fans can treasure the memories of more than a century's worth of baseball glory as they await that next pennant.

INDEX